Under the Influence of

Under the Influence of

Lilacs

Deborah Gordon Cooper

Clover Valley Press, LLC
Duluth, Minnesota

Clover Valley Press, LLC
6286 Homestead Rd.
Duluth, MN 55804-9621
USA

Cover design by Stacie Whaley, i.e. design
Cover and interior art by Joel Cooper

Printed in the United States of America on acid-free paper.
Library of Congress Control Number: 2010923897

ISBN-10: 0-9794883-8-9
ISBN-13: 978-0-9794883-8-2

Acknowledgments

Many of these poems were first published in the following publications: *ArtWord Quarterly, The Roaring Muse, Kalliope, Wolf Head Quarterly, North Coast Review, Minnesota Monthly, Nimrod, Rosebud, Dust and Fire, the gods of wild things* (Poetry Harbor), *Redirection of the Heart* (New Song Press), *Response* (Calyx Press), *The Moon Rolls Out of Our Mouths* (Calyx Press), *Between the Ceiling & the Moon* (Finishing Line Press), and *Trail Guide* (Calyx Press).

The author thanks the beautiful, brilliant, and irreverent women in her writing group for their wisdom and encouragement: Candace Ginsberg, Ann Niedringhaus, Ellie Schoenfeld, and Anne Simpson.

for Joel,
the one who walks beside me

Contents

One - New Poems

~ *Two* ~ Between the Ceiling & the Moon
(Finishing Line Press, 2008)

~ *Three* ~ The Moon Rolls Out of Our Mouths
(Calyx Press, 2005)

~ *Four* ~ Redirection of the Heart
(New Song Press, 2002)

~ *Five* ~ The Gods of Wild Things
(Poetry Harbor, 2002)

~ *Six* ~ Between the Branches
(Power of Poetry, Dominican School of Philosophy & Theology, Berkeley, CA, 2001)

One

New *Poems*

Prelude to Daybreak

I am the scarlet ribbon
on the rim of sky,
behind the penciled lines of trees

prelude to daybreak,
the first strains
of a symphony.

Across the city
and the countryside,
eyes turn

on the way to the barn
or the bus

through the windows of kitchens
and trucks

of waiting rooms
and penitentiaries.

I am a glimmer of
the answered prayer

the chance of hope,
the promise honored.

I am why you set
the newspaper aside

step out the door,
breathe deeply in.

The Sparrow

This morning, I pray only
for the sparrow on the deck

not for peace, or cures
for ravaging diseases

just this one precise petition
for this one particular bird

stunned, sudden collision
with the window glass.

I keep vigil for an hour
until he finally flies away.

Tomorrow morning
I may ask for something more. ⁀

Threshold

Some changes take you
like an undertow.
Gasping for air,
you thrash against the pull.

Others you choose,
and still, the struggle.

Think back…
you have been practicing this step
inside some hidden room
within you
for the longest time.

How often have you dreamed
this threshold?
The key dissolving
in your palm.

Today, you are awake.
Reach out your hand,
the slightest touch.
The door swings wide. ⌐

Green

I am the color green
your eyes crave.

Late March,
by now the pines
are insufficient.

I am that half-remembered
tender-green,
color of longing

curled in the earth
'til the first inkling
of thaw

asleep in the deep
of a frozen pond,
a promise in my throat

I am on my way to you. ¬

Waking from Grief

The fog over the water thins,
the sheerest voile,
distills the light.

Here, an altar at your feet,
the stump of some long-tumbled oak
brimming with tender shoots,
delicate leaves
like tiny, upturned hands.

The trees along the beach
cannot contain themselves,
this soft explosion
of new-green. ⌐

Matins

I sit on the wooden bench
above the bay
the way someone
somewhere else
sits in a pew.

The waters whisper
in the mother tongue.

I read poetry
the way someone
somewhere else
reads scripture.

Letting the book fall open
where it may,
seeking some shard of light,
enough to see by. ‿

Instructions

Leave your cell phone, your watch
and your thoughts
on the kitchen table.

Walk slowly.
Leave the trail

to follow a scent
or to follow a bird's refrain.

Stop often, and listen
for the under-sounds.

Notice what grows at your feet,
the puzzle pieces of the sky
and what the light reveals.

Cast out your gaze like a net
and take everything in

every intricate detail,
each small astonishment. ⌐

Under the Influence of Lilacs

The buds of lilacs split
their tiny seams

unleash their fragrance,
lifted by the breeze

through window screens,
through yards of summer-children.

A woman, dozing
in a rocker
on a porch,
dreams of a long-ago lover.

Her husband,
watering the garden,
begins to whistle an old song.

Birds call and answer
in the branches.

A man walking a dog
stops, caught in the memory
of a lavender dress.

And someone, somewhere,
starts a poem. ─

Already

For the first time
since I was pregnant

for the last time,
twenty years ago

I go three months
without bleeding;

start taking brisk walks
against a gnawing in one hip

though I am easily
distracted by

a kite, caught
in a tree

an orange bird
I cannot name...

the way the lilacs
have already
turned to rust. ⁔

Lately I've Noticed

alone in the house
or in the car,
occasionally over produce
at the market,
I talk aloud to myself
as if I am a friend of mine.

And I'm reminded
of the old woman
in the old neighborhood
(how old was she really?)
alone in her garden,
nattering on and on,
the lush garden,
the disheveled house,
the house I'd always run
my fastest by.

And still, I keep catching myself
addressing myself out loud
as if I am my constant friend,
a friend who often tries my patience.
"Please," I snap unkindly,
"I just need my space."
Offended then, I pout
for half an hour. ⇁

Looking Out

At some point then,
inside herself,
she must have turned around
without noticing
until today

looking out of the same red window
she'd been looking out for years,
every morning

into the same field
framed in gorse;
the same road
scribbling its way away
into the village.

But when had she begun
to daydream
in the mornings
looking out

about what was already over
instead of what might come…
the music prize she'd won;
the summer Albert loved her?

As if the possibilities
that had once filled
her thoughts

that she might move away
and play the violin
or even marry

had been blown out
like a row of candles
one by one,
no matches in
the drawer. ⌐

Yellow Flowers

All winter, the winds rage
across the hills

thrash at the cottage
where she tosses
in the quilts

rising in the dark
to feed the peat-fire
passing the days with the weight
of a cold, dark stone

in the center of her chest,
the accumulation of sorrows.
The weeks crawl by.

But now today,
beneath the breeze-swept
clouds and trees

the yellow flowers
are opening their faces

a throng of tiny trumpets
blaring Spring

a galaxy of fallen stars.

For eighty years, she's watched
these flowers shine
in their brief season

and felt each time this small, familiar
half-forgotten
shock of joy. ⁓

Woman

She has borne witness
again and again

felt the ravaged earth
beneath her feet
and heard the children cry.

She knows the way the dark
can take the light
without a warning

a candle snuffed out
in a sudden gust

the whole sun plunging
from the sky.

She knows that what we hold
won't last,
be it a blossom
or a body.

She has borne witness
again and again

and still, her gracious face
takes everything in

and still, her arms are open,
and her hands.

She has borne witness
again and again

and still, she rises. ⌐

October

The rain is undressing
the trees

gently,
no sense of urgency.

I open wide
the window

the scent
and song

of falling rain upon
the falling leaves

cascade of memory

so that I stop,
put down whatever
I am holding

the dish towel,
the pen,
the wooden spoon

and I walk out. ⌐

After the Fall

The fragile bodies
of the fallen leaves
are curling in upon themselves

curling in around their own
small shadows

a pose I recognize,
that inward turning,
curling in around the heart

the heart
thrashing in its cage,
after the fall

the fall, the call in the night,
the night that will go on and on,
the night you only want to wake from. ~

Gift from My Brother's Wife

I ask gently,
knowing how hard it is
for her to part with
his belongings

if someday I might have
one of his shirts
or sweaters.

The next time I visit,
tea in the fall garden,
all the flowers winding down

she lifts a sweater from the line,
the Irish one
I'd often seen him wear

washed by hand
and hung in the sun to dry,
a loving gesture

yet I stumble on my thanks
and hope she doesn't notice.
She folds it carefully.

I hold it to my chest…
wanting to press it to my face,
wanting to breathe in
any trace of him. ¬

The Other Jubilee

Because grocery shopping
in a city this size
is a social event

a conversation across cantaloupes,
a bit of gossip over grapes,
self-disclosure in the coffee aisle…

because for weeks
following my brother's death,
I wore my heart
on the outside of my body,
like a brooch on my coat

any bump or nudge
could fall me;
any mundane question
send me reeling
for the door…

I shopped on the other side of town,
drove ten miles out of my way.
I made no eye contact. ¬

The Winter Following
My Brother's Death

I am waiting
for the amaryllis
to wake
from its thick sleep

waiting to see
the first shoot loosen
from the knotted bulb

a green hand reaching
for the light

the shroud beginning
to unravel,
one tight thread
at a time.

Late Winter Day

At last, the sun succeeds

wearing a hole in the fabric
that drapes the sky.

I am waiting
for the gray cloak of winter

and of grief
to ease

freeing my shoulders,
unburdening the breath.

Afternoon stretches
into evening

leaving, overhead,
a web of lace.

The blue shows through. ¬

While You Are Away

I do your laundry for the first time in years,
since that squall about your socks
when the children were small.

I smile at the way
your boxers tangle
with my bra.

Ironing your favorite shirt,
the fabric thinning slightly
at the elbows,
the collar threatening to fray

I think, for the first time,
how much I love your elbows,
how dear to my hand is the perfect
back of your neck. ⌐

My Valentine

I have had the same Valentine
for thirty-five years.

That first November
when we started going out

I asked if he would be
my Valentine.

It was a trick question,
and I have had him ever since.

Rarely has he brought me the flowers
I am perpetually hinting at.

"Joe gives Mary a dozen white roses
   every year," I say.

He smiles vaguely
and goes back to his book.

Quite often, he gives me
a box of the chocolate turtles
he so dearly loves

and only once, kitchen utensils.

Watching him now
outside the window,
ten below,

blowing the driveway
in the dark

then tossing salt
across the sidewalk
where I slipped

I know, again this year,
he is the one. ¬

Winter Evening

I am this luminous blue,
edging towards cobalt…

the interlude between
the sun's dip-under
and the dark.

I am the shade that stills you,
that calms the whir and reeling
of the mind.

Just this,
the deepening blue,
a string of heartbeats
and the breath.

I am the whole note, held
before the curtain falls

before the stars are tossed
across the sky. ¬

After You've Gone

I find you in my hands
upon the piano keys.

I wear your ring.
I memorize your poetry.

I see you in the colors
at the edge of day

in every opening
and closing.

I tuck your rosary
in my pocket

wrap myself up
in your pink shawl…

and still. ¬

Grocery List

Lettuce, tomatoes, onions,
green beans, strawberries

and I am swept back
to the farm in summer

sweet juices trickling down
the children's chins.

"You can eat one for every ten
you pick," I'd tell them,
but they were cheaters.

Bananas, grapes, apples
and peaches

and I can almost taste
my mother's pie.

What has become
of all her recipes?

The Jimmy Carter cake,
the Christmas-shopping stew,
the Scots meat pie?

Gone, along with questions
left unanswered.

Paper towels,
toilet tissue, Puffs.

Why, as a child,
would I hear her cry
behind the bathroom door? ⌐

Constellation of Two

I light a candle
on the piano

search the sky
for any evidence of you,
returned to stardust.

Venus rising,
a beacon in the deepening blue

to keep her vigil
through the night.

I make a wish
for the impossible…

for you belong again
to light
and not the body.

The evening star grows brighter
with each inch.

The candle flickers
in the jar. ⌐

Remember Your Way Back

not as far back as the night
you sat beside the dwindling fire,
beneath a sky spun out of stars

and believed that everything
was possible.

Remember your way back

not as far back as the day
the letter came in the mail,
or perhaps it was a package

an answer to the wishes
that you'd made with coins and candles
and a whispered prayer

that ephemeral glow…
before your heart scrabbled
for the next thing.

Remember your way back

perhaps an April afternoon,
the polished blue of sky,
the sculpted shoreline

the dappled patterns in the water,
water that lulled you
to a reverie…

and you thought,
perhaps you even spoke the thought
to the one who walked beside you

the one who
in that moment
took your hand

"Imagine this might be eternity."

Imagine that it is. ⌐

I Think of You

Because the sun's decline
behind this sheet of cloud
reminds me of music

the way the colors bleed
across the parchment of the sky
like a crescendo.

I stir the embers
of the dying fire.

Now, high above the fallen sun,
one slender strand
of orange lingers
like a descant

and I remember you
beside me here,
singing the notes of the stars
on the staff of the sky

when time was still one piece,
not split into before
and after.
Adagio…

the day's last light,
a final chord,
fades from the sky.

But then,
the bright staccato
of the fireflies.

I think of you. ¬

Shattered Gardens

Here, soft breeze
rustling the canopy of maples.

Dew, like jewels
strewn through the grass.

There, a boy in uniform
sleeps fitfully,
gun at his side

a boy who once slept
with a clown-doll
to keep bad dreams away.

Across the square
another boy
straps on a bomb,
recites a prayer.

Somewhere a mother
lights a candle.

Here, bright bits of birdsong
fill the air

and there, the wailing
of a father,
falling,

falling
to his knees. ⌐

Morning Paper, Mourning Prayer

Let us pray for the born children.
Let our prayers lift us to our feet.

Let us pray for the born children.
Let us take not another moment of silence,
but let us raise our voices now.

Let our prayers be the works of our hands,
the inclination of our hearts.

Let our prayers be hope &
sweet, unbroken dreams.

Let our prayers be soup & bread
& rice & oranges.

Let our prayers move us out of pews
into the villages & shelters.

Let us pray for the born children,
the children sleeping now
inside the house next door,
the children sleeping on the streets,

children in Israel & India & Palestine,
the wounded children in Iraq.

Let us pray for the born children.
Let us pray that we might cease
to plant the seeds of fear
& hatred in their minds,

that we might never lay
another weapon of destruction
in their arms. ～

We All Wake to the Same Sun

the woman in the brownstone;
the man in the trailer
at the end of a dirt road;
the boy sleeping in the dumpster,
seeking refuge from the cold.

We live and move in this same
circle of light,
crossing the sky and sea,
the walls and barricades
and borders.

We whisper the same prayers
in a thousand tongues…
Peace.
The safety of our loved ones.
Peace.

We all shelter the same
small flame of hope.
We all come to know
the weight of grief.
We hold our children close.
We hold the old ones.

We see beauty
in a single yellow flower…
in a field or in a child's hand;
through the barred window
of a cell.

We hear beauty
in the music of a nightingale,
a lark.

All over the world
we join our voices,
singing the way open
in every language,
singing the shackles free.

In different countries,
bells or drums
call us to prayer.
We bow.
We kneel.
We face the four directions…

the same praise in our mouths;
the same needs in our hearts.

Night falls the same way everywhere,
the deepening blue,
the dusk,
the dark…
upon the hungry and the fed,
the loved,
the lonely.

We dream the same dreams everywhere,
inside a tent,
a penthouse
or a high-rise.

Sleep beneath the same soft moon,
the same tossed scattering of stars.

We all wake to the same sun. ⌐

Two

Between the
Ceiling and the Moon

By Moonlight

She has lived alone so long
in the old farmhouse,
grown up here
and let her family go,
one by one, into the city
or into the earth.

Days go by without a word.
Her voice, when she must use it
on the odd trip to the market,
startles her,
as does the phone
which rarely rings now,
the cat's infrequent meow.

Nighttimes, she wakens
to the hum of silence.
Her practiced ear
can hear beyond
the slight breeze weaving
through the cottonwoods,
beyond the barn owl,
beyond the frenzy
of the field mouse.

She can hear the grasses shiver
in the moonlight,
the creak of ancient apple trees
beneath her window,

souls murmuring
in the overgrown orchard,
arias
in the full face
of the moon.

What We Keep

As instructed
by my grandmother
at ninety-eight,

hoarder of small things,
scraps and baubles
filling drawers…

"They'll come in handy someday,"
she would say…

I save things too,
the way a child
tucks found treasures
in her pockets.

Last night, I chose the soft
lavender ring around the moon,

today, the call of loons
across the bay,

the great blue heron
rising in the slough. ⌐

Abandoned

Swimming from sleep,
he reaches out across the bed.

He sees her slippers,
still tucked beneath the chair.

He is now so easily bruised
by any ordinary thing…

wisps of curls, caught
in the bristles of her hairbrush,
left on the dresser.

He can almost see her there,
the back of her neck
asking for his lips.

He drinks his coffee
at the window
by the kitchen sink,
safer there than at the table.

He sees a pair of finches at her feeder
and turns away.
Yesterday, it was the peanut M&Ms.

He left his half-filled cart
abandoned
in the candy aisle. ⁓

Tikkun

(Hebrew for: mending the world; raising divine sparks)

The man with the overloaded grocery cart
insists I go ahead of him.
Did he see me looking at my watch?

Even though I'm running late,
I take the time to help the stooped woman
wrestle a bag of dog food to her trunk.

Arriving home,
she calls her daughter on the phone,
as if they'd spoken only yesterday,
never mentioning the rift.

The daughter's husband
walks through the door
into an embrace.

Later, unasked, he cuts the grass
of the widow down the street.
From the window, she waves,

feels brave enough now
to sort through Frank's things,
pick out a keepsake for each grandchild.

Three states to the east,
the gay grandson, long estranged,
opens the package, unrolls the bubble wrap,
carefully hangs the mirror on the wall.

Stones they had collected
from that rocky shore
when he was small

set in the frame by his grandfather's
steady hand.
That night, he writes a letter. ⁓

Between the Ceiling & the Moon

My mother's hand
miscalculates her mouth.
She keeps jabbing the cookie
into her chin.
"Are my teeth in?" she asks,
as if this might be the problem.

Last week she told me
she'd been stuck up
on the ceiling
for the longest time.
Today I hang a string
of tinfoil stars
above her bed.

The circumference of her life
is pulled tighter
with each round of the clock,
like a knot,
like a seed
that will break open
elsewhere.

And still, she asks
each time I walk into her room,
"Has the baby come yet?"
and something loosens
in my chest.
My daughter is serene & round
& luminous,
as if she had swallowed the moon.

Now the moon
is following me home…
the new moon,
holding the shadow
of the old…
the old moon, graciously
giving itself up. ¬

Rooms & Furniture

"We have only the present moment,"
someone says again.
Again, I disagree.

The moment that
I open up her hands,
curled now into tight fists,
rub lavender lotion
into her thin skin,
a drawer unlocks in me…

and we are playing
our sonata,
my fingers on the high part
never quite catching up
to her hands,
two perfect dancers
on the piano keys.

Rocking my daughter's baby boy,
I slip through a door
into the made-up song
I sang when I rocked her.
Same scent of baby skin.
Just down the hall,
my father's whistle
joins me.

We are filled with rooms
and furniture and hallways,

trapdoors
and windows, looking out
into the distance up ahead.

Sitting here
on my end of the couch
writing

and watching you
between the lines

sitting there
on your end of the couch
reading

that window opens
where I know
someday
one of us will be gone.

A teeter-totter tips, as if
one kid's jumped off.

I stop the poem
and lean toward you,

lift the book
out of your hands. ˹

Sorting Her Things

Never mind about the piano
and the china.
Never mind about the rocking chair.
I want the rosaries,
and I will fight you for them.

I want the Saint Theresa one,
made out of rose petals,
the one carved out of Connemara marble
and the one made of Venetian glass.

I want the crystal one
she took when Nana died
and always kept beneath her pillow.
Some days she'd wake,
Hail Marys tangled
in her hair.

I want the one she gave to Dad
the day that he became a Catholic
so she'd marry him
and he could go to heaven too.
These wooden beads feel warm
between my fingers.
Just to hold them
is a prayer.

When I was small
he'd thaw my winter fingers
in the sandwich of his hands,
cupped to his mouth,
three warm breaths. ~

Imagine

Patting your back,
your back no bigger than my palm,
coaxing the bubbles up,
that happy milk-drunk look upon your face

I start singing whatever
comes into my head
(John Lennon's "Beautiful Boy")
to garble the tough talk
on the TV.
The news is always a mistake.

Your little back, my little drum,
I sing "Imagine."
I couldn't have imagined
when this song was new
that by the time you came around,
first baby grand-boy,
we'd be handing you the world
still unrepaired.

I want to take you to the woods.
I want the trees to be your teachers.
The white pine and the maples
and the mountain ash, growing up
out of the same patch of earth
shoulder to shoulder, roots entwined.

All over the world, your sisters and brothers
are springing up…
first breath, first light,
first arms to hold them.

You burp, bobble your head
and fall asleep.
Your life is right here
in my hands. ⁓

For Drew

In the picture
you look out of your face
the way you always did,

a look that could make anybody feel
they were the one
you had been waiting for.

Sweet gap
between your two front teeth,
plaid cap,

traces of laugh lines
at the edges of your eyes.
They will not deepen.

I pray for a dream
where you play again,

the music running through you
from some other world.

Each note,
a bright bird lifting
from your hands. -

Time Change

Driving back & forth
to the city, again & again,
torrent of tasks & details
on the heels of death,
I am betrayed
by the bare bones of trees,
the fleeing geese,
the grasses, fading
in the field.

Home, I reset the clocks.
I shop for candles,
set the tabletops ablaze
a little earlier each day.
I put Drew's music on.
At first it wounds;
at last it comforts…

as does the music of the chickadees,
still singing their summer song
though the sky threatens snow
and the long winter looms.
Across the yard,
the solace of the evergreens,
the oak that won't let go
its burnished leaves,
the golden tamaracks. ⌐

Solace

And still
the world goes on
being beautiful…
the trees, the water and the sky
offering solace,
whether we see or not.

Just now, the clouds
behind the black limbs
of the mountain ash
catch fire in the last light
of the day.

Hope rings
in the delicate throat
of a single bird,
singing the sun down,
whether we're listening
or not.

Even as we sleep
the gracious moon
traces the sky
keeping the night-watch,
soft spill of light
across the bed. ~

Three

The *Moon Rolls*
Out of Our Mouths

The Writing Group

When we arrive,
our arms filled with poems,
you, in the next booth,
might want to move off
to the table in the corner.

At first glance,
it might appear that
there are five of us.
At second glance,
a crowd.

We are the soldiers
sent to war,
the small girl
maimed by a bomb.

We are the rain
waking the memory,
the wind, coaxing the clouds
across the sky,
lifting the white lace
of a curtain.

We are the cat
curled on the bed,
the robin in the yew bush,
God in a tutu,
French-blue lilacs in
an alabaster bowl.

The moon rolls
out of our mouths.
The dead rise up between
the pages in our hands.

The Yellow Skip-hop

In the woods, a small bird
asks me to follow him,

skip-hops ahead then stops,
waiting for me to catch up.

Surprise of yellow
when he lifts his wings.

I used to worry that I didn't
know the names of things,

bought every field guide,
mushrooms & butterflies & trees,
but I always seemed to forget.

Now I just make up my own names.

This bird, after all, doesn't know
what they call him either.

At first I wonder where
he might be taking me,

some secret spot where I'll
receive a message or a sign?

Eventually I realize
we're just hanging out

among the sunswirls and
the purple Nana's-hats. ˢ

River Dreams

Through the darkest season,
dreams of the river carry us.
Current of memory...
the teahouse skirts
the rapids.

The sky, along that
far side of the year,
holding the light.

Shadows of white pine reach
the evening's edge,
fragrance of cedar trees.

Nothing unbidden falls
upon our ears,
just this

intricate ecstasy
of water,
pure, uncomplicated
glee of birds. ~

This Step

Somewhere
around the middle of your life

you understand that
it is not the destination.

Nor is it what is waiting
where the road turns next.

It is the step that you are taking now,
or maybe what has stopped you.

It is this soft light, sifting
through the leaves,

the red-winged blackbird
calling from the mountain ash.

It is the secret whispered
in this breeze,
this breath. ⌐

All Saints

For weeks now
the light will keep leaving us.

As if in compensation for the sun,
I light a dozen candles.

I rearrange the faces on the piano,
trace a finger down my father's cheek

which is covered with dust,
making me feel like a negligent daughter.

I still hear his voice in the odd dream
and from the mouths of my brothers.

I wipe his face with my sleeve,
his face, stuck in the same expression
day after day.

Nana's jaw must ache with smiling
after all these years.
Grandad, forever looking off to the side.

One by one,
the faces in these photographs
become the faces of the dead,
my secret saints.

I light a candle
for each one of them,
as if the piano were an altar,

play my Nana's favorite hymn,

flames quickening
with each chord. ⌐

Things I Didn't Know I'd Miss

The way his hair
those last few years,
precisely Brylcreemed
through my childhood,
sprang from his head
like a flock of startled gulls.

Watching from the window,
before the wandering began,
when he could still find
his way around the pond,
circling for hours if
we didn't bring him in;
the day I realized he had put on
mother's lilac coat,
her white angora gloves.

The day, wanting to help
as I made lunch,
he set the table, using all the
family photographs as plates.
Ham-on-rye on his
Canadian Air Force face. ⌐

Behind Each Window

they land back
in their beds,
the gauze of dreams
falling away.

Here and there
a strand, still tangled
in a woman's hair,
or wound around the fingers
of a small boy's hand.

The mind
in those first upright moments,
returning to the jungle
or the stranger's face
then losing hold,

fastening itself back,
putting the water on for tea.
These mugs that will not be
turned into birds,
thrilling the hand,

the table that keeps its shape;
the house across the lane,
set in the same gray
puzzle of stones
as every other day.

Soon, the first door will open.
The first person will come
around the corner

the way he always does,

briefcase and lunch sack
in the hands
that have lost the memory
of the reins,

the feel of the sweat
on the muscled neck
of the black horse. ¬

Winter Storm Warning

The sky is packed with
sack-of-flour clouds.
I know that I should go now
in the nick-of-time
to Super One
with all the wise Duluthians
stocking up

but this mauve afghan,
the one that Nana knit,
has pinned me to the couch.
Later, craving stew,
eating the last two crackers in the box,
I will, along with all the other slackers,
call Domino's
and tip big. -

The Dancers

With the first turn
of that first dance
sixty years ago,
they turned into one of those couples
that does everything together.

Now they are forgetting
together.
She loses words.
He loses keys and wallets
and his way.

"The armadillo has five red blooms,"
she beams. He calls the police,
certain he's had his pocket picked again.
Then later, when she finds the wallet
safe upon the closet shelf,
he blames the cleaning crew.

"I can never get this phone to work,"
she shouts. He rushes in to save her,
patiently punching the buttons
on the remote, holding it to his ear.
"Must be the battery."

And yet, each time the music starts,
they tango or they samba
or they jitterbug.
They never miss a beat. ⹀

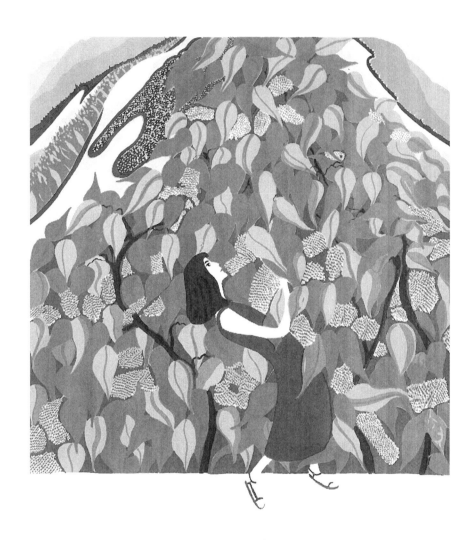

Four

Redirection of the *Heart*

Just Before the Turning

When day begins to lean
towards night,
that earliest inclination,
a pause of breath, the redirection
of the heart...

The woman
taking clothes down off a line
presses her face against the flannel
of a shirt, breathes deeply in.

Across the lane
the fragrance of the lilacs
lifts a neighbor from her kitchen
through the screendoor
to the yard,
the branches reaching out their hands
brimming with blossoms.

The old man, in his garden
down the street,
seems to be listening for something
far away.
He floods the marigolds.
While from an upstairs window
someone watches him,
his daughter or his wife, hand
at the curtain.

When day begins to gather in
the light

each kind of passing
seems to show itself...

a holding, and
an opening of the hand,
as if the two
might be one gesture,

as if, in certain moments,
we might long for
what we have. ⌐

The Letter

My father, who can't remember
what he had for lunch
or if he's eaten anything at all,
tells me that once
trying to win my mother's heart
he had made a letter
out of flower petals
and sent it to her in the mail.
He must've been nineteen.
And I imagine him, unfastening
the daisies from their orbs,
undoing blue-bells and
reorganizing asters.

My mother remembers then too.
Remembering makes her face go soft
and shine right on him
in a way I have not seen
in years.
And I can see her, opening
the envelope that day,
the same look softening her face
as if a breeze had crossed it.
Somewhere, out of sight,
a gate swings open. ⊸

Waiting

It seems
she has been waiting for you
all her life,

the months that you were missing
in the war,
your plane plucked from
the German sky.

Every day she prayed to St. Theresa
for your safety.

She made a pact with God
that she would never eat ice cream
if she could have you back.

Married then, at last,
she kept on waiting for you,
living in one room
without a piano

while you studied medicine.

You told her
you were driven by the war
to learn a way of
mending damages.

And, in the one
small closet,

red high heels
with straps, the ones
she loved to dance in,
waited too

beside the box
with all her music
packed inside.

I wonder
while she waited,
having babies back-to-back,

pregnant with me
when Greg was only three months old,
with no piano
and no ice cream,

I wonder
if she ever wondered what
she'd gone and done

or if she thought of Walter Lavender
at all, the boy who danced
like Fred Astaire,
the boy she'd left
to wait for you. ~

Practicing

My father only wants to eat
Eskimo-pies.
I bring a new box every Sunday.
He leaves them, melting
and forgotten, on the couch,
between the pages of the books
he cannot read but carries everywhere,
as if they hold his old identity.
My father can no longer tie his shoes.
He waits for me to,
sitting meekly in the chair.
I remember sitting on the stairs
of the old house
while he taught me how,
before kindergarten, on the day
of the shoe scramble.
I swallowed my crying then too,
afraid that it would be too hard.
I tie carefully, the way he
taught me, making the laces
even, using double-knots.
He is talking, something about the sky
outside the window
and the war,
loses hold of the thought,
dozes off between words.
I look up at him, his face
collapsed against his chest, traces
of chocolate on his chin, slipping out
of the world, as if he is
practicing leaving it. ∽

Reasons

Because there is so little
left blooming,
each delinquent petal
seems to shine.

Because the sun is pulled
behind the hills
a little earlier each day,
I wake in time
to catch it rising.

Because my father
is forgetting
how to talk,
I make a treasure
out of every
awkward utterance. ⸜

The Benevolent Doorman

Because, growing up,
I'd heard you say

"Pneumonia is the old man's friend."

I recognized him
when he came for you. ⌐

Trust

The trees on the cliffs
are teaching us everything.

They cannot fathom what it is
that makes us cling
and cower.

They lean out,
standing on their toes,
as if light were the truer gravity

as if the pull of earth
were some old superstition
we might rise above

as if there were
some wider watchfulness

as if we could spin ourselves wings
just as easily as falling. ⌐

Sardines

When I was growing up
I pretended to love sardines
because you did.

We'd share a tin together,
line the silvery fish up
on saltines.

The boys would gag, and
I would roll my eyes at you
and wonder if I fooled you.

Once, after a sleep-over,
I pretended to like
pancakes and syrup
and ate a whole stack

because I knew
that Cathy Collins' mother,
standing in her bathrobe
at the stove

had lost her hair
because of cancer.

Later, when I threw up
on her bathroom floor,
I cleaned it up myself

and stuffed the towel in
the bottom of the hamper.

After Cathy's mother died,

I thought that certain lies
might not be sins,
not even venial ones.

Once I pretended to forget
that it was Friday

until I had eaten
the whole hot dog.

Then I pretended
to remember.

I wasn't sure
if I'd fooled God.
I didn't think that I'd
fooled you,

but you pretended
that I had.

Today I eat half the tin
of the sardines

I had been saving
for your birthday,

the King Oscars,

laying them out in careful pairs
on the saltines,

trying to look as if
I'm loving every bite,

just in case you might
be watching now. ⌐

Visitations

On Tuesday, in the produce aisle,
choosing my oranges by feel
and by their fragrance,
I hear my father whistling in my ear.
A Scottish lullaby.
Everything else stops.

There is a tenderness no border can contain.
A web that may be glimpsed
in certain, unexpected plays of light,
or felt, like a shawl
across one's shoulders,
laid by unseen hands.

There are sounds in other decibels
the heart can hear, when the wind is right
and the mind has quieted its clicking.
The border guards are sleeping
at their stations.
Spirits come and go.

The wall between the living and the dead
is as yielding as a membrane,
is as porous as a skin.
Lay your palm against it
and you can hear their voices in your hand
and in the place where the chest opens
like a flower.

They are not far away,
no farther than the breath
and enter us as easily,
in pine and peonies,
in oranges and rain. ⁓

Five

The Gods of

Wild Things

In the Picture

there's a child
that you cannot see.

It can be a boy
or a girl,
whichever you choose,

of that age where the limbs
grow long and lean

and urgent with a need
for running.

This child hides
behind the banyan tree,

sneaking from Sunday school,
commandments set in stone.

In a moment,
the very moment
that you look away,

this child will dart
across the page,
fly to the sea,

preferring the gods of wind
and dunes and wild things,

the gods of the fish that slip
from the nets, free. ¬

Tintinnabulum

She is grateful for the bells
calling her back.
She can never pay attention
the whole time.
Sometimes she tries,
running her finger
down the lines.
Red words for the priest.
Black for the pew-sitters.
But her eyes are always tugged up
to the colored windows,
the candles dancing in their jars,
souls of the dead,
the sad, chipped face of Mary.

She is grateful for the bells.
One   Two   Three
Because that means this is
the holy time,
the God-coming time,
the time not to be daydreaming.
The whole crowd
falling to its knees,
like a tipped ship.

Sometimes she shuts her eyes
the way her father does,
hopes God might notice her.
Maybe God will whisper in her ear.
One word, unlocking everything.

Later she begins to hear the bells
in the wrong places.
In the woods
or lying in the grass
when she is cloud-watching.

The first time she lets her blind cousin,
Linda, "see" her face and dress
with her fingers,
she hears the bells.

And later,
when she sees her busy mother
in the garden
lean to kiss
the purple petals
of the irises,
she hears the bells again.

Soon she begins to make
her own small prayers,
printing them neatly
with the red pen
in her diary.

"The bells are in the garden
and the wind.
The bells are in the fingers
of the blind girl's hands." ˜

Gazing

Sitting on the couch
in the warm nightie
Hannah gave me for Christmas,
I watch you jam your legs
into your jeans,
tug on your boots,
tromp through the snow,
because of the way the light
lands on the ice floats.

The lake heaves and shrugs
like an animal,
trying to shake off
what wants to pin her down.
Mid-January now
and she is not locked in.
I root for her
and you, standing
fixed above the bay.

"What are you doing?"
I would ask at the beginning,
poking through your trance.
"I'm gazing," you would say,
as if it were your job
to memorize the world.

You haven't taken
your gloves or hat.
That increment of time
could cost the perfect
slant of light.

Now something else
has caught your eye.
You head off down the path.
Who knows how long
you will be gone now.

For thirty years
I've watched the way
you watch the world,
as if you were blind
in some past life
and must make up for it,
as if every morning
you'd been given back
your sight,
as if they'd just unwrapped
the bandages. ¬

Collecting Light

I see the way the chickadees
take turns at the feeder.
I watch a neighbor take
her husband's hand.

I see the way the sun will find
the only interruption
in dark clouds
to toss this amber light
across the pines.

I see a row of cars
stop on the road
until the orange cat
has safely crossed,
then take off slowly, should
she change her mind.

I watch the way my brother
lifts our mother from
the wheelchair
to the car,
the shawl he lays
across her lap.

I save up every scrap
of light,
because I know that it will take
each tiny consolation
every day
to mend the world. ¬

Three Love Poems

1.

"We can't leave dad alone,"
my mother tells me on the telephone.
"Remember, Mom?" I say,
"Dad died a year ago."
"I know that," she snaps back.
"I just don't want to
leave him by himself."

We've had this conversation
every night this week.
I pour myself a second glass of wine.

Last night, she was considering
divorce.
"He just ignores me
when I talk to him."

2.

This morning Madeline calls,
crying, missing Kent,

and I recall the way it feels
to be apart at twenty-two.

"At least he's not dead,"
I think of telling her,
but say instead,
"Every day apart brings you one day closer."

This wisdom doesn't seem
to be the slightest comfort.

3.

This afternoon,
arriving at the cottage,
I leave the groceries in the car,
rush in to call you at the shop,

because of the fox
in the yard,
and the first irises.

I let the phone ring fifteen times,
then try back every fifteen minutes.

In the hours before you finally call,
with such an ordinary explanation,

I've imagined every manner
of calamity…
how can I tell the children?

fretting that the last thing
I had said to you was,
"Aren't you ever going
to cut that grass?" ~

This Morning

I see the first geese
leave us.
The children have
moved south too,
leaving their closets
jammed with stuff
they have no room for
but cannot throw out.

One day I tried,
but the one-eyed elephant
stopped me.
I set him in the rocking chair.
She'd told us, Christmas morning,
that she'd meant a real one.
That's why she'd written it
in capitals,
A ELEFANT
a pair of skates.

The trees are just
beginning to turn.
Here and there
a maple bears
a single torch.
Already we
with instincts of our own
are stacking logs
against the cold.

Sitting high above the lake
upon the bench we made
in memory of my father,
I feel him, across
a wide distance,
as if he were standing
on the other side
in Canada.
A broad-winged hawk
glides by. ~

Before

Sometimes
beginning to burn

a log in the fire will sing,
remembering the birds.

A brown bowl
holding three tangerines

holds too, the memory of
the hands that shaped it

and holds the cool,
still silence
of the earth.

Each tangerine
repeats the image
of the sun.

The shadow
that the rocking chair
releases

dances on the wall
like a tree,
answering the wind.

In the dark
we slip, with the breath,
out of our sleeping bodies

into all we knew before. ⌐

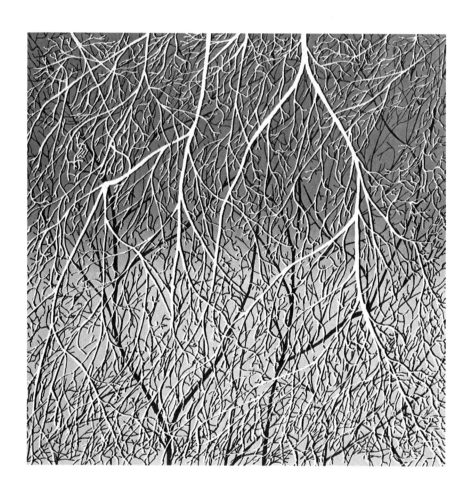

Six

Between the
Branches

Blackthorn Trees

At first they fool us,
the blackthorn trees
on the Irish coast,

bending in rows
like dancers,
delicate and fragile
in late light,

dark lace against
the grace of evening sky,
leaning in unison.

Up close
they tell another truth,

twisted and bristling,
a mad tangle of branches,

their backs long crippled
by the winter's
unrelenting winds.

The only kind of tree
that has survived
this landscape.

The fists
of these roots
have not loosened their grip
across the centuries.

And every spring
they lash back, in rages
of white blossoms.

This Bed

For more than half of my lifetime
I have slept here, in the crook
your body makes,

our breathing
mingling in the air
above this bed,

bought, in the beginning,
at an auction,
bidding more than we had in the bank,

the tall, carved headboard
like a treehouse
in a forest.

No matter how wide
our separate days might open up,

the night invites us
to this tender resolution,

falling softly through
the rims of dreams,

reaching, it seems
even against our waking wills,
for one another. ⌐

In the Dark

Lying beside you
in the dark,
I make of myself
a small boat
and drift away.
No matter where
night lets me go,
I know I'll wake
against your shoreline.
Each pushing off's the same,
across whatever distance,
the bed,
the city,
or the sea.
Our hands
tied in a soft knot,
our arms,
like kite-strings,
keeping the way back. ⁓

Far Away

across the dark arc
of the sky

I want to think
you're thinking of me,

sitting in your favorite chair,
an open book, forgotten
in your hands.

I want to think your hands
are wanting me,
my skin imagining your touch,

my eyes remembering
your eyes,
looking at me.

Somewhere along the line
that spans the distance
in between us

my thoughts of you will find
your thoughts of me

and bloom in the night
like a new star
beneath this half-a-moon,

this moon I want to think
you might be looking at
right now

outside the window
by your chair,

thinking of me,
across the dark arc of the sky,
writing this poem for you. ⌐

Feeding the Fire

Here you will find
everything you need.
There is no e-mail
and no telephone.

There are the waves
playing leap-frog
for the shore;
the wind's long fingers
combing through the trees.

Here you only need
to feed the fire
in the hearth
and in your own soul.

All afternoon
you watch the gliding gulls,
until you know the way
to send your messages
as easily.

Aim one toward Canada,
then Cleveland,
then the Isle of Skye.

Imagine them arriving
at their destinations,
coming to rest
upon a shoulder
far away.

Across the world
a pair of eyes
lifts from the page.
The snow begins to fall
outside the window. ～

The Daughter

Now that he is dwindling,
going down
for the third time,
thrashing
in the tangle of the sheets,
she comes from far away
to care for him.

She wipes his face,
tips tiny sips of water
in the sunken cave of the mouth
that spit the battering words at her;
washes the hands
that sent her running
for the woods.

Once, she lay
beneath the maple tree
all night,
prayed for a fire
to come and take him.

Today, she rubs his feet
and scrubs the kitchen
of the trailer
where he's lived for years
alone,
at the dead end
of a dirt road;

hauls in the wood
that keeps him warm.
She is making things right,
repairing,
in the only way she knows,
the holes
he's left inside her. ¬

Correspondence

In a soft fold of time
between the ironing
and the income tax,
I think of Nana's red rose tea.
I see the subtle tremor
of her hands,
the china tea cups
rung with strands
of tiny violets.
I hear the small song
of the silver spoon.

I'd like to think
my thinking of her
might arrive,
that sudden pulse of love,
surprise her at her window
in the way a sparrow, rising
in a breeze,
catches her eye;
the way a neighbor
lifts the ordinary morning
with a wave. ⌐

Between the Branches

It was always snowing
when I visited.
Remembering, I see you
again and again
opening the door,
and then your face
as if it mattered that I came, as if it
made some kind of difference after all.

You'd offer tea
and one day, worrying that I was cold
coming out of my boots,
you gave your rag wool socks to me
to wear, warm from the radiator.

Each time I came
there was less of you waiting,
less hair, less fullness to your face,
less energy.
Only your elaborate eyes increased,
taking my breath away.

Sometimes we'd meditate.
The animals would join us.
Or you would let me read to you,
Audre Lorde or Mary Oliver.

I thought that there would be
more time,

that spring might come
and we might see a bit of it begin
before you left us.

Every now and then
I find myself looking for you.
Just now, between the branches
of the birch, I catch the rich
mosaic colors of your eyes,
but then the clouds close. ⌐

Transients

We are just passing through
these bones,
the way this wind
inhabits the ravine,
the way this light, in its
allotted time, illuminates
the hollow.

We are just passing through
these bones,
folding and opening
these limbs.

We work these hands,
making our sandwiches
and love;
look out at one another
from these faces,
watch a raven
trace the sky. ⌐

Whatever Is Lost Here

Finding the smooth,
black stone,
the one you will keep
in your pocket,

you imagine it, tossed
from the rocks
of that far country

by the hand of
your grandmother's
grandmother.

Whatever is lost here
will turn up again,

a thousand miles away,
a hundred years from now,
on someone's shore,

a dream,
a bone,
a doll, caught
in the tide;

the tangled remnant
of a rosary;
a ring, flung
from a bridge. ￢

The Hidden Waterfall

Coming from a world
where planes collide

and every doctrine's
full of holes

and boys pack handguns
in their lunch boxes,

to find, two miles back
into the woods,

this water, falling
like a curtain of light

across the black
geometry of stones

seems to change everything.

Simply to know that here,
in the middle of nowhere,

there is something so
unreasonably beautiful;

simply to know
that when I leave,
my whole soul quieted,

this water will keep on
weaving its gauzy light
across these stones

even if I never find my
way back here again. ⌐

About the Author

Deborah Gordon Cooper has been writing poetry for twenty years. Her work has been published in numerous literary journals and anthologies, including *ArtWord Quarterly, The Roaring Muse, Kalliope, Wolf Head Quarterly, North Coast Review, Minnesota Monthly, Nimrod, Rosebud,* and *Dust and Fire.* She and her husband, Joel, who is a printmaker, have exhibited their collaborative images throughout the Midwest. Deborah has used poetry extensively in her work as a Hospice Chaplain. She co-edited the anthology: *Beloved on the Earth: 150 Poems of Grief and Gratitude* (Holy Cow! Press, 2009), and she frequently teaches writing classes for those who are grieving the loss of a loved one. She conducts workshops on the interfacing of poetry and spirituality, and has mentored inmates at the St. Louis County Jail. Deborah is the author of four previous collections of poems, most recently *Between the Ceiling & the Moon,* published by Finishing Line Press as part of its New Women's Voices Series.

CPSIA information can be obtained at www.ICGtesting.com
Printed in the USA
BVOW010342171012

303178BV00007B/52/P